BRITAIN IN OLD PHOTOGRAPHS

DORKING REVISITED

KEITH HARDING

SUTTON PUBLISHING LIMITED

Sutton Publishing Limited
Phoenix Mill · Thrupp · Stroud
Gloucestershire · GL5 2BU

First published 1997

Cover photographs. Front: Gadbrook Farm, Betchworth, *c.* 1910. Back: High Street, Dorking, *c.* 1870.

British Library Cataloguing in Publication Data

A catalogue record for this book is available from the British Library.

ISBN 0-7509-1652-4

Typeset in 10/12 Perpetua.
Typesetting and origination by
Sutton Publishing Limited.
Printed in Great Britain by
Ebenezer Baylis, Worcester.

Howard Road, Dorking, looking towards Ranmore, *c.* 1870. Constructed between 1852 and 1870, Arundel and Howard Roads provided well-proportioned houses for the middle and artisan classes. The Arundel Arms closed in the 1980s. (Photo: J. Chaplin)

CONTENTS

Rose Hill archway, Dorking, looking towards South Street, *c.* 1870.

INTRODUCTION

I bought my first camera when I was nine years old. It was a small plastic affair with a flip-up wire viewfinder, a kind of first cousin once-removed of the spud-gun. They must have been close relatives because they were both to be found in the toy department of the Reigate Woolworths. Not that this was a toy, you understand; costing 2s 6d this was to me the real McCoy and what is more it represented a sizeable chunk of my disposable income. When it was loaded with a roll of 126 Verichrome Pan I had twelve frames to last me the whole of my two-week summer holiday in Mousehole. And last me it did. But then I only took photographs of really important moments, like the three mackerel we caught from the boat in the bay or my new best friend Edwin throwing stones at the tangled masses of seaweed or my brother tossing bits of a cheese sandwich to whirling seagulls. One frame of each, no wasted film and if it worked, it worked.

Those photographs were taken for one simple reason – to record a precise moment in time. Once the shutter had fired that moment was captured on film, never to return. It was history. The photographs that appear in this book were taken with the same intent, not to create history, just to capture a moment in time. It is that moment that can eventually become the subject of historical interest. When John Chaplin came over to Dorking from Guildford in 1870 with his mahogany and brass field camera, he had little notion of recording historic detail; his intent was to make a profit from the sale of photographic prints, for the science of photography was still in its early stages and not readily available to all and sundry. Cameras for the masses were still several decades away and the period until then was filled by images taken for the spectacularly successful picture postcard market. Photographers the length and breadth of the country were taking photographs to satisfy the insatiable demand that was created for this cheap, efficient and, above all else, illustrated form of communication. It is only because these postcards were as eagerly collected as they were dispatched that we have what is now an invaluable form of pictorial history. For an age that has become bombarded by visual images of dazzling technological sophistication it is a sobering thought that we put such emphasis and attach such importance to simple photographs taken a century ago that were carrying no underlying messages, just recording that small moment in time. With this in mind I have strived to find contemporary written accounts relating to these images in order to give a more authentic impression of how the people of the day viewed their everyday lives and surroundings. So much has changed in such a short period of time. Different values, ideals, expectations and viewpoints all contrive to render our opinions in such a different way from those of our forebears two generations since. With one week to go before the deadline arrived for this book I found a postcard in a dealer's box in Canterbury that showed the belfry of the church in Newdigate. Looking at the message on the back I discovered that it had been written by one of the craftsmen working on the tower in 1906. This man's simple message added new life to the caption that I had previously written describing the restoration of the church. A simple statement of fact has become a poignant record of history – thanks to the postcard.

The photographs taken on my real McCoy camera forty years ago were not supposed to be making an historic statement but in another forty years time maybe someone, somewhere, will see my 'study' of three mackerel and exclaim 'Cor! look at this' . . . but then again maybe not.

Keith Harding, September 1997

ACKNOWLEDGEMENTS

Many people have helped in the production of this book, giving freely of their time and knowledge and lending photographs, without which some chapters would have appeared very lean indeed.

My thanks to: Caryl Brain, Malcolm Covey, Mary Day, Victoria Houghton, Mary Mansell, Ted Molyneux, Kathleen and Stanley Pierce, Margaret Whitfield, Dorking Museum.

Hand-printed and sepia-toned photographic copies of the illustrations used in this book are available from the author at the address below. Readers may be particularly interested to note that, with the kind permission of Ted Molyneux, prints are also available directly from the Chaplin glass-plates of c. 1870. These, too, are hand printed, toned and mounted by the author at: Goodness Gracious, Jayes Park Courtyard, Lake Road, Ockley, Surrey, RH5 5RR, tel: 01306 621474.

ABINGER &
HOLMBURY ST MARY

Friday Street, Abinger, c. 1912. This famously picturesque area was a popular picnic destination for the Edwardians, but the family in this photograph are, in fact, the wife and children of Percy Lloyd, noted photographer from Albury, who very often incorporated them into his wonderful postcard photographs. In the 1900s bathing in the pond was permitted 'before 8 and after 8'.

Friday Street, Abinger, *c.* 1920. Friday's Cottage, on the left, was Dixon's bakery which delivered by horse and cart to the district. In the period between the wars an old railway carriage was put to further use as a tea-room in the garden of the cottage.

Abinger Hatch, *c.* 1905. Offering six bedrooms and three rooms on the first floor, the inn was well placed to cater for coach and charabanc visitors, hikers and 'excursionists'.

 'The comfortable old-fashioned inn, though remote from towns and railways, is probably well known to professional new and "brain workers" as any house in Surrey. There is nothing of the modern hotel, but good English fare, old ale, and other liquors suited to the requirements of hungry men and women who are spending their day of rest on foot, amid beautiful scenery, breathing fresh air and laying up a little store of health for the days to come. About luncheon time they appear from all directions, and presently vanish again; each group on their separate way towards London. Though the Inn is known as the Abinger Hatch, the coat-of-arms on the sign board is not that of the Abingers, but, I am told, the Tankerville-Chamberlaynes.' (J.S. Ogilvy: *A Pilgrimage in Surrey*, 1914)

St James's Well, *c.* 1900. Built by the local company of King, at Abinger Hammer, for the Lord of the Manor in 1893, the well descends to a depth of 150 ft.

Abinger Bottom, *c.* 1910. In this remote hamlet a spring rises, the stream from which runs through Friday Street and joins the Tillingbourne at Wotton House. At one stage the building in the centre of the picture was a bakery.

Ellen Smith recalled: 'Some traces of isolation in the more remote wealden villages can still be detected in the lingering superstitions, peculiar speech and habits of the people, though railways have done much to remove linguistic and other peculiarities. Perhaps the least advanced people in the whole area are those living in the deeply furrowed region north of Leith Hill. One is astonished to find here people to whom the luxury of a coal-fire is unknown. They are free to take as much wood as they can carry themselves from the neighbouring coppice-land, and one may see in spring the women and children of these little communities busily carrying the faggots home.' (*The Reigate sheet of the one inch Ordnance Survey*, 1910)

Abinger Hammer, *c*. 1912. Erected as a memorial to Thomas Farrer of Abinger Hall by his wife Euphemia in 1891, this is the second clock to occupy the lofty site, the earlier one having been removed to Abinger Hall Stables. The figure of the blacksmith was carved from teak by a Burton-on-Trent company that specialised in carving fairground gallopers.

Abinger Hammer, looking east towards the post office, *c*. 1905. On the left are a pair of cottages built in 1745 as Scudgers, now known as Marsh View. Opposite the post office is the yard of W. & G. King, the local builders founded by William King, wheelwright, in 1836.

Abinger Hammer, *c.* 1905. These cottages were built for workers at the Coe brothers' watercress beds, which was the first large-scale business of its kind in England.

Abinger Hammer, *c.* 1904. The postman on the tricycle is outside the earlier post office (now Grasmere) and is heading towards the former wheelwright's shop, now the forge. What appears to be a railway porter stands on the left, presumably from Gomshall station.

Abinger Hall, *c.* 1908. The Hall was built in 1783 by Capt. Matthew Pitts and much altered by the 2nd Lord Abinger. The Estate boasted an elaborate water pumping system whereby a water wheel, driven by the Tillingbourne, pumped water from a bore hole to a reservoir on Abinger Roughs, which then gravity-fed cottages on the Estate. The house was demolished in 1959.

Abinger Hammer School, *c.* 1906. Built in 1873 and run by the County Council since 1909, the school is now funded by community and friends and administered by the Abinger Hammer Village School Trust, which was formed in 1982 to save the school from closure.

Sutton, Holmbury St Mary, *c.* 1905. The Volunteer was originally a beer shop known as Seaman's Garden in the mid-1800s. In 1886 the Guildford brewers Lascelles and Tickner acquired the property. 'The Volunteer, a quiet little tavern, served mostly beer from a small sanded bar, and part of it was a shop presided over by Mrs Wells, the landlord's wife. Everyone had to obtain their water from a dip-hole in the stream running in front of the Inn. Each summer, probably early August, the little field in the centre was the scene of an annual Fair.' (*Holmbury Parish News*)

The green, Holmbury St Mary, *c.* 1905. G.E. Street's 1879 church, built of Holmbury stone and dressed with Bath stone, dominates the green, upon which the village held an annual fair on the first Wednesday in July. This was a professionally run event and held to be a red-letter day in the village calendar. 'We were grateful to hear about Mr Cory, the proprietor of the steam round-about used at the recent Fair on the Green, when he thoughtfully softened down the music in order to disturb as little as possible those who are lying ill in cottages near the Green.' (*Holmbury Parish News*)

Felday chapel, Holmbury St Mary, *c*. 1905. The early nineteeth-century Congregational chapel tended the religious and educational needs of the ancient hamlet of Felday. A small school existed in the chapel prior to the building of Holmbury School in 1868. 'I always feel that historically the most interesting building in the village is the tiny unpretentious Congregational chapel, half hidden away among the trees on the hillside. This modest and architecturally unattractive little building dates back to the old "Surrey Mission" of the Congregationalists. It was part of a sincere and praiseworthy effort to provide facilities for worship in portions of the wilds of Surrey, which had 'till then been neglected by other religious bodies.' (E.A. Judges: *Some West Surrey Villages*, 1901)

The green, Holmbury St Mary, c. 1910. The grocery store on the green moved to that site in the 1920s after the Surrey Trading Company had acquired the business started by Mr and Mrs Sykes at the White House. For many years the shop ran as part of Forrest Stores group, but it is now a private residence.

The Glade, Holmbury St Mary, c. 1905. On the left stands the woodyard that belonged to local builder Henry 'Buffy' Amey. It is reported that he encountered financial problems owing to the poor quality of the houses that he built in The Glade. The Amey family came to the village in about 1800.

The Glade, *c*. 1910. The pair of cottages on the right were built in 1864 by Henry Amey for £100 each, and in 1909 Percy Ovrington ran a cycle repair shop from nos 1 and 2, later expanding the business to become a garage, seen lower right.

'The things we most remember of old Holmbury are the swarms of gypsies on the common pestering us to buy pegs, or begging for food at our doors; the unadopted road (The Glade) deep with mud, leading to their camps – "the bottom" as it was called then; trudging to school through that same mud.' (Miss Collinson recalling 1892, *Holmbury Parish News*)

The Glade, *c*. 1905. The little hut in the centre was the workshop of Charles Penfold, broom and brush maker, who was supposed to have been blinded by an exploding lemonade bottle.

'The actual open land at Felde Bottom (now known as The Glade) was grassed. It was free of weed as it was well grazed by locally owned horses and particularly by the gypsies' horses. Scotch pines grew down almost to the backs of the houses. Red squirrels lived in the tall trees, existing on the seeds of the cones. There were three better class houses but the rest were owned by the gentry who lived under Holmbury Hill and were tenanted by estate hands, building craftsmen, gardeners, etc.' (A. Strudwick, *Holmbury Parish News*)

The Glade, *c.* 1910. Clereholt, on the right, was originally two small cottages and the present house was started by Mr Potts at the turn of the century. On the left are Old Burchett and Holly Cottage, built in the 1880s to house servants from Joldwynds, the mansion nearby.

The Women's Institute Hall, *c.* 1930. Constructed by the Abinger builders W.G. King at the southern end of The Glade and enlarged in the 1970s, it has become the focal point for village activities.

Feldemore, Holmbury St Mary, *c.* 1905. Edwin Waterhouse, founder of the international accounting company Price, Waterhouse & Company, bought some land in Felday called Cooper's Copse (Feldemore Woods) in 1877 and engaged George Redmayne to build Feldemore in 1882. He then purchased plots of land in all corners of the village, erecting buildings whose number and design changed the whole appearance of the village and its way of life. Feldemore is now Belmont School.

Pitland Street, Holmbury St Mary, *c.* 1910. The hamlet of Pitland is shown on a 1762 map as being a cluster of six or so dwellings named Pedland, and Neale Cottage dates from about 1618. The King's Head, on the right, is probably seventeenth-century, and at the time of the photograph was owned by Lascelles and Tickner, the Guildford brewers.

BEARE GREEN & CAPEL

The post office, Beare Green, c. 1905. William and Lizzie Geary moved into the post office in 1906. It was also the village store, selling anything from pots and pans to leather boots, which were hung from the ceiling. Before the Gearys, Fred and Michael Dean operated the original post office from the timber 'shed' (in centre of picture) before moving on to Newdigate. Arthur Voice, the postman, lived in one of the cottages on the left, which the Gearys bought in the 1930s for £250 the pair. When William Geary died in 1951 his daughter, Kathleen, ran the shop for another five years, after which the business closed.

The Mission Room, Beare Green, *c.* 1905. Like so many rural areas, Beare Green had its 'Iron Room' church-cum-meeting place. This stood close to the forge on the green until it was moved over to the other side behind the cottage named Puffins next to the post office. It continued to be used for regular church and Sunday school meetings until destroyed by fire in the 1960s.

The cricket ground, Beare Green, *c.* 1903. Beare Green once boasted its own cricket team, which played regularly on the green. They had no pavilion or changing area, so the players had to arrive dressed and ready for action.

The forge, Beare Green, *c.* 1910. Standing on the edge of the green, close to the road, is the forge, which at this time was operated by Mr King, farrier and blacksmith. It ceased functioning just before the Second World War, and is a private residence today.

The Street, Capel, looking from north to south, *c.* 1917. Seventeenth-century Yew Tree Cottage on the left faces Orchard Cottage, which was once known as Capel Boot Stores. Behind the baker's cart is the carriage house to Brockholt, with Hurst Cottage in the background.

The Street, Capel, *c.* 1910. The second house from the left was for many years the baker's shop. In 1832 Thomas Goacher traded there, followed by names such as Tilt, Berry, Stent, Barrett, Carpenter and Christmas. In 1980 Beatie Griffiths (*née* Christmas) recalled: 'I well remember the winter of 1927 when around Christmas time we had the heaviest fall of snow I can recall. A double-decker bus skidded into the drain by the Misses Hodsoll's farmhouse opposite and couldn't be moved for two days. I helped on the bread round as conditions were so bad. We had a high "tip-cart" in those days, which held about a hundred loaves and smalls inside, with the flour box and baskets on top. This had a tarpaulin cover in wet weather.'

Just beyond are Britannia Cottages, which were refurbished in 1892 for workers on Churchgardens Farm by Charles Mortimer (at Wigmore).

Aldhurst Farm, Capel, *c.* 1905. The name seems to be derived from the 1382 landholder Aldous Clerhole. The building in the centre dates from the early sixteenth century and there have been many additions. The left side dates from 1885. The Dales, a Quaker farming family, have been at Aldhurst since 1826 when the property was rented from the Broadwood Estate, and they finally purchased the freehold in 1991. William Nash recalls the Quaker meetings of 1851: 'Our meeting – Capel – was but small; two families, the Sargents and the Dales, the latter being like the Sargents, such a nice old-fashioned kind family, but oh! so serious looking. From the youngest to the oldest, we never could fancy that they had ever been laughing, playing infants. There were also two non-members, father and son (Millers, I think); they came in well-oiled boots, snuff coloured leggings, most beautifully white smock-frocks, soft yellow silk handkerchiefs round the neck, and beaver hats, one, if not both brushed wrong way to show the beauty of the beaver staple.' (William Nash: *A Surrey Memory of 1851*)

The Street, Capel, 1950. Behind the wall lies the school, built in 1826 and enlarged in 1872. The shop next door was built in about 1845 for Joseph Nash – grocer, draper and farmer. Percy Teasdale ran the store from 1931 to 1976 and recalled: 'I arrived in 1936, no gas, no electricity and everything fairly black with the oil lamps.' In 1939 he purchased the freehold for £921 1s 6d.

St John the Baptist Church, Capel, *c.* 1905. The chief part of the present church was built in about 1240 and much of that work remains, despite alterations and additions. The last major work was in 1864 when the south porch was rebuilt, a north aisle, organ chamber and vestry added and an arcade of four arches built to replace the north wall of the nave. There is a peal of six bells in the wooden, shingle-clad tower, the oldest having been cast in 1593. Close by the entrance is an ancient yew tree, estimated to be 1,700 years old.

Chennell's Garage, Capel, *c.* 1910. The first mention of F. Chennell is in 1899 when he traded as a carrier, later as a coal dealer and then as a 'motor and cycle agent, repairer and garage'. He traded at this site, opposite the Friends' Meeting House, until 1932.

Wigmore, Capel, *c*. 1910. In 1866 Charles Smith Mortimer, a company director of Mordern Park, Surrey, acquired the land which became Wigmore Estate, purchasing two farms, Sprots and Rugge, and built his mansion on a 'fine commanding spot'. On his death in 1892 his son, also Charles, enlarged the house and estate to 1,000 acres, including Hoyle, Hillhouse, Capel House, Ewekene and Church Gardens farms. Fifty farm cottages were modernised and some of the farm houses were let as private dwellings, and in 1898 the cottages on Misbrook Green and the Red House were built. Charles Mortimer died in 1924, by which time much of the land had been sold, leaving only Sprots and Rugge.

Bennett's Green, Capel, *c*. 1905. The Methodist church was built in 1876, thanks to the vastly increased numbers of followers who outgrew the small room near the Friends' Meeting House. The first minister was Mr Sewell, stationmaster at Ockley, and the hall at the rear of the church was added in 1904. On the right are Rose Cottages, one of which housed builder David Mitchell in the 1880s. His diary records: 'March 9th 1886 – Hard frost, work at school. W. Wright taken for stealing a cake at Stents.' 'March 31st 1885 – Fine day, frosty morning, went to Temple (Elfold), rabbit hunting, killed 374.' Rawson Cottages, which now stand where the telegraph pole is sited, were built in 1911.

Methodist Chapel, Capel, *c.* 1905. 'The railway extension from Dorking to Horsham was opened on May 1, 1867. One of the new stations was Ockley. The station-master, Mr Sewell, was grieved to find that there was no chapel either at Ockley or Capel. Services were held in Mr Groombridge's cottage (Oakwood Hill), and a few Methodists employed in the brickfield near Ockley station, and others living in Capel, walked over to Oakwood Hill now and then. . . . Mr Sewell formed a night-school for the young people, and then invited them to a Sunday morning Bible class. The response far exceeded his expectations. The young people were asked to bring their parents to a service in the station house. Every available chair had to be used, and the largest room was filled. The station-master conducted the service, and the people begged that it might be held regularly.' (*Methodist Recorder*, 1903)

  A cottage with a large room attached was rented from Mr Jeal for £20 per year and the cottage sublet for £8, with services held on Sunday mornings and afternoons and on alternate Tuesdays. These were sufficiently well attended for it to be deemed necessary to build a chapel, and the present building opened in 1877 opposite the room used originally for services.

Grenehurst, Capel, *c.* 1920. John Sheldrake is known to have been at Greenhurst Farm in the 1860s and it is on this site that William Cazalet built his mansion in 1870, staying there for thirty years. The house went through a succession of owners until 1965, when it became the Elim Bible College, providing 'training for young men and women with a call to specialised Christian Service in Great Britain and overseas'. In 1990 the building was substantially altered and extended to provide apartments, and much of the gardens used to create new, detached housing units.

Capel, *c.* 1910. Roger Carter came from Norfolk and set up a business shoeing horses with his partner Isaac Baxter in the 1870s. They embraced new technology and began to sell, repair and even make bicycles. Roger's son, Archibald, took over and in 1906 he walked to Dorking to purchase a car manufactured by the splendidly named Alldays and Onions Pneumatic Engineering Company, Birmingham. Soon after, petrol was being supplied in 2-gallon cans and the business diversified into retailing hardware. Ray Carter took over from his father in 1935, with his sister Dolly running a tobacconist and sweet shop next door, and these businesses later merged. Neil Carter succeeded his father in 1965, and it was he who re-developed the site in the 1970s. Neil is due to retire soon, and after more than a century someone other than a Carter will be running the business.

Shiremark Windmill, Capel, *c.* 1935. The first appearance of a mill on this site is on a map of the manor of Dorking in 1649. In 1774 Shiremark smock mill was built partly from salvaged material obtained after the demolition of Clark's Green Mill, and in 1802 it entered the possession of the Stone family who held it for many years, together with Bennett's (Bonet's) Farm, and it was under the ownership of George Stone when it last worked, in about 1914. Gradually the structure decayed and by 1956 it was in a pitiful condition, all the sails having fallen off. In the 1960s the mill was gone, leaving Outwood as Surrey's sole surviving working post mill.

The photograph shows harvesting at Bonnett's, and Maurice Markham, who came there in the 1930s, recalled: 'At this time (1942) two elderly farm workers were still with me, men who had spent a hard working lifetime in the fields and woods hereabouts, gifted beyond measure. Whether their knarled hands were working with a hoe or axe, they demonstrated skill and craftsmanship of the highest order. These two – Snip and Joe Chennell, members of a well-known Kingsfold family – walked to work each day from their cottages adjoining the Dog and Duck, using footpaths and bridleways, through Tickfold, Wattlehurst and Bonnett's Farm to arrive never a minute late and ready to do what was to hand that particular day. I took Snip and Joe to this field of once-proud wheat. It had beaten the binder, but not those two old country men. Tools were found and sharpened, then coats off and dinner bags stored under an ancient oak nearby the field gate, a quick swig of cold tea and away they went. Their sickles crackled as the over-ripe straw was gathered into sheaves.'

'Near Bonet's, perched on a windy knoll on the county boundary is Shiremark Windmill, now, I think, the only one of these at work in Surrey, and it is a pleasure to watch the swift revolution of the great sails, to hear the creak of its beams, the hum of the millstones, and to see the miller dusty with his toil.' (J.S. Ogilvy: *A Pilgrimage in Surrey*, 1914)

BETCHWORTH &
BROCKHAM

The Street, Betchworth, c. 1905. A lone boy stands on the path that leads to the school. At this time there was provision for 188 pupils in four classrooms, the largest of which had places for fifty-six. On the left of the picture is the entrance to Home Farm, which was worked by the Constable family from 1881 to 1923.

More Place, Betchworth, c. 1915. The home is probably fifteenth-century in origin, and was probably built for Thomas and Alianora Morsted, whose son Thomas was surgeon to Henry V. This photograph shows the house in about 1915 shortly after the death of the tenant, James Corbett, who had spent fifty-eight years at More Place, during which time he and his wife Julia became deeply involved in village life. James Corbett was a churchwarden for fifty years and Julia trained the choirboys, cared for the sanctuary and even carved the choir stalls and panelling at either end of the altar.

Hartsfield, Betchworth, c. 1910. This house was built in the 1860s by Arthur Jaffray, who died before the house was completed. His twenty-three-year-old widow was pregnant with their daughter, Mary, who lived at Hartsfield until her death in 1936. After short periods of occupancy by the Higfords, Lloyds and the Army, the building was turned into a residential hotel, later becoming a staff training college for Midland Bank. Currently it is a conference and training centre.

The Dolphin Inn, Betchworth, *c.* 1905. Until recently this eighteenth-century building belonged to Betchworth House Estate. A room was set aside on Quarter Days for the collection of rents by the agent. Frank and Emily Bridger raised eight children here in the late 1800s, one of whom, Frank Jnr, ran the pub until 1930. The Dolphin is widely considered to have been one of the last inns in Surrey brewing its own beer, production ceasing in 1926.

The Dolphin Anglers' Club, *c.* 1900. Frank Bridger Jnr took over the running of the Dolphin Inn from his father in 1900 and founded the angling club at about this time. The fishermen are pictured alongside the River Mole, just below the Dolphin.

St Michael's Church, Betchworth, *c.* 1905. The building is of Saxon origin with thirteenth- and fourteenth-century windows. The whole tower was moved from the centre of the church in 1851 to its present position having become unstable, possibly owing to repeated excavations at its base to inter bodies. 'It was then removed bodily to its present position, much to the bewilderment of students of archaeology, who, without knowledge of what was done must find the plan a very difficult one to decipher.' (*Victoria County History of Surrey*)

Betchworth Fire Brigade, *c.* 1900. The hand-drawn fire pump was housed behind the double doors next to Forge Cottage, and manned by a volunteer brigade as was common practice at that pre-motor vehicle time. At the rear, left to right, are: Tom Arrow, Tom Basset, Frank Short, Bill Short, Bill Judd and Jim Arnold; seated are William Fuller and Ernest Stovell.

Old Road, Betchworth, *c.* 1910. On the left stands the butcher's shop, whose occupants have included Toop, Beall, Lilley and Hodgson, the latter moving into a new shop at the top of Brockham Lane in the 1930s. The other buildings depicted are Elm Villas, built in the 1870s, and at the far end, Roffey's grocery store, started by Charles Roffey, who could trace his family back in parish records for over 200 years.

Betchworth Chalkpits, *c.* 1906. The North Downs have provided lime products to the building and farming industries for centuries, but it was the building of the railway line linking Reading to Redhill in 1849 that saw the Betchworth works grow to become one of the principal sources of employment for village men. Standard gauge tracks connected the works to the sidings north of Betchworth station. 'The enormous chalk-pit proves that by constant digging, man can move mountains, for it has now reached the crest of the hill.' (J.S. Ogilvy: *A Pilgrimage in Surrey*, 1914)

The lime works, Betchworth, *c*. 1910. Thirty-nine lime workers sit around the easily distinguishable figures of Sidney Nightingale, works manager, and Miss White, the typist. The family names of Barnes, Webber, Botting, Wren, Fuller and Boniface are still to be found in the village, and many of these families originally lived in the sixteen houses called New Cottages built in The Coombe in 1876.

Betchworth station, *c*. 1905. The Reading to Reigate branch of the South-Eastern Railway opened in 1849, affording the village a link to trains bound for London. This attracted many of the city's business and professional classes to the area. The sidings to the south of the line were used by the coal merchants and for the delivery of agricultural supplies, while the sidings to the north-east of the station were used for loading and unloading sheep, many of which came from Romney Marsh to be fattened on the farms hereabouts.

Old Reigate Road, Betchworth, *c*. 1909. A butcher's cart and a telegram boy pause outside Tranquil House, which served as post office from 1880 until 1900 when the present building was completed by local firm Geo. Cummins & Son. The wooden footbridge across the road linked Broome Park to its walled garden and was raised to allow double-decker buses to pass safely underneath. It was later removed altogether.

Station Yard, Betchworth, *c*. 1905. 'E.A. Kirby Livery Stables – Coal, Coke & Woodmerchants, Carmen & Contractors': so read the signs on the building that stands south of the railway, adjacent to The Beeches, built as a railway hotel in the 1850s, but soon to become a private residence.

Gadbrook Farm, Betchworth, *c*. 1910. Jabez Swan and his family farmed here for fifty years following their arrival from Wiltshire in 1906. He was also a mainstay of 'The Brethren', who held meetings in the chapel at Gadbrook, carrying out baptisms by total immersion in the pond in front of this farm on 'Dipping Sundays'.

Snower Hill House, Betchworth, *c.* 1910. The DuBuissons came to live at Snower Hill in about 1880 and raised six children there. They were reputedly the last family in the village to use a brougham, and this affectionate snapshot taken by the youngest of the children, 'Peggy', shows the coachman Ellicott, dog Mischief and the horse Dolly.

Wonham Mill, Betchworth, 1898. Edward III granted rights of Wonham Mill to the priory at Reigate in 1328 and eventually the mill became part of Wonham Manor in 1678. Michael Bowyer and his family tenanted the mill from 1845 to 1930. After the Second World War the Ministry of Food used it for grain storage. Here William and Charlotte Kempshall stand by the mill pond with William (b. 1891) and Rose (b. 1892)

Wonham Mill, 1898. William and Rose Kempshall hug one another, poignantly, at the front door of the Mill House at Wonham. A few months after this photograph was taken, William went out to play in the garden as usual, yet when his mother called him in there was no response. She searched the neighbouring meadows to no avail, and returned to be met by her distraught husband, who had discovered young William's body, drowned, in the mill flash. Rose became a headmistress.

Wonham, Betchworth, *c.* 1900. A very carefully posed team of labourers stand by their wagon in a field at Wonham. 'In the old days hay was mown with the scythe, and made with the fork and rake. Sometimes there was a large three-pronged wooden fork – a tool of great antiquity, but later used only for barley; and the farmer had a wide drag-rake with iron teeth. But for the actual needs of hay-making there were but three tools – scythe, fork and wooden rake.' (Gertrude Jekyll: *Old West Surrey*, 1978)

Brockham Lane, *c.* 1930. The lane was built on land purchased from the Deepdene Estate in the late 1920s. The old willow trees, now over seventy years old, are gradually dying and being replaced by new trees planted just inside the Field, which is now a sports ground.

The Borough, Brockham, *c.* 1900. These buildings fronting the River Mole are all of early origins and stand above the flood level. Plots of land leading down to the river were offered for sale in the 1930s, but the scheme foundered when anxious villagers warned the potential buyers of the risk of flooding.

Brockham Green, *c.* 1925. A charabanc is seen passing along Old School Lane while a canvas-topped lorry makes a delivery nearby. The single-storey building at the centre of the photograph was for many years occupied by the cobbler Mr Godding and before that Mr 'Bill' Bailey.

Brockham pump, *c.* 1930. The pump was erected in 1862 as a memorial to Henry Thomas Hope, Lord of the Manor from 1838 to 1852, and paid for by public subscription, the total cost being £39 19*s* 6*d*. The original plan was to erect it over a spring in The Borough, but investigation revealed a blocked up spring on the green so the drinking fountain was sited at that point.

Old School Lane, Brockham, *c.* 1905. The Old School was built on land given by Henry Thomas Hope of the Deepdene, Dorking, in whose memory the village pump was erected. The 'new' school was built in Wheeler's Lane in 1871.

Old School Lane, looking north to Dolly Farm, a seventeenth-century building with additions, *c.* 1909.

Looking north from The Leighs, Brockham. The cottages on the left of the photograph line Old School Lane and were built in 1847 by a local man, John Harman. The name The Leighs (pronounced Lyes) refers to that area of ground between Old School Lane and the church.

Elm Grove Farm, Brockham, *c*. 1900. A timber-framed building with Victorian cladding and additions, the farm formerly belonged to the Deepdene Estate.

Brockham Green, looking towards Old School Lane, *c.* 1906. The large house in the centre, Brooklands, built in the 1850s, was the home of architect Henry Bowman. The lectern in Brockham's Christ Church was presented by his widow, Sarah, in 1893. Behind the pump stands the eighteenth-century building Birch Cottage, for many years the home of the Sherlock family.

Brockham Green, *c.* 1913. For centuries the village green has provided the centrepiece for any local celebration, and cricket matches were played here until the 1960s. The striped tent belonged to Mr Sidney Poland, a London furrier who was a great benefactor to Brockham, bringing slabs of fish from Billingsgate on Friday afternoons, providing boots and shoes for the needy children and sending many of them for a week's summer holiday to Ramsgate. The Poland Trust still administers the distribution of small amounts of money to children, who sing carols at Poland's Corner on Christmas Eve.

W. Harman's bakery and general store, Brockham, *c.* 1920. William Harman was a member of the long-established Brockham and Betchworth family. The shop is now Surrey House and stands to the north of the village hall. Trade ceased in 1928 after the suicide of William Harman.

Home Lane (Wheeler's Lane), Brockham, looking north towards Way House, *c.* 1905. The two pairs of wooden buildings on the right date from the 1850s.

Brockham Home, *c.* 1909. In 1859 Mrs Way of Wonham Manor founded the Brockham Home and Industrial School for poor orphan girls aged eleven to sixteen. They were trained in all aspects of household work to suit them for domestic service and they were provided with a home when no position was available. There was a resident matron and a schoolmistress, for the girls did not attend the village school until 1871.

Home Lane, Brockham, *c.* 1905. In 1872 Mrs Way founded a home for fourteen infants with a resident matron, and this later merged with the home for older girls under the care of one matron. The enterprise was managed by a committee of eleven ladies and the chaplain, the Revd Alan Cheales. The matron lived in the house at the rear. Wheelwright's Cottage on the right is seventeenth-century and was lived in by the Skeltons.

Christ Church, Brockham, *c.* 1870. This church was consecrated in 1847 by the Bishop of Winchester as a daughter church of St Michael's, Betchworth. The then oldest inhabitant, Johnson Batchelar, aged eighty-eight, recalled: 'I remember well the first Sunday the Church was opened for divine service. I, hearing the bell tolled, opened the front door and saw the Revd John Miller, of Ipswich, walk straight down the middle of the green to C.W. Roworth Esq., the appointed churchwarden, in his black silk surplice and I thought what a fine sight for Brockham and the rising generation. It caused such a thrilling sensation in me that I can never forget.' (K.M. Dodson: *Birth of a parish, Christ Church, Brockham*, 1988) (Photo: J. Chaplin)

Oakdene Road, Brockham Green, *c.* 1915. This development of late Victorian houses could only be approached from Wheeler's Lane until the 1950s, when a bridge was built over a stream enabling the road to connect with Middle Street.

COLDHARBOUR
& LEITH HILL

Coldharbour, c. 1905. 'The houses are mostly of stone or concrete; the roofs and halfway down the sides being covered with thick red tiles, which give them a very pleasing appearance. The village straggles along from Anstey Lane to Mosse's Wood but its greater portion is clustered near The Plough. A little below, though on higher ground is the school, the smithy, some private houses and the Post Office which is also the general store of the village. Facing the Post Office is the village green, devoted to cows and cricket.'
(Dorking and Neighbourhood, *1888*)

The Plough, Coldharbour, *c.* 1925. At the turn of the century the villagers met socially at the parish church room and on occasion used a large building in the yard at the Plough. After the First World War a brass band was formed and they used the building for practising. In 1909 Henry Lipscomb, landlord of the Plough, built Hill View chiefly as apartments for summer visitors.

Coldharbour, *c.* 1905. Right of centre, in the distance, stands the school, built in 1910 to replace the 'free' school of 1819. The school closed in 1965. In front stands the smithy and along the road is Henry Roffey's shop and post office.

Coldharbour, *c.* 1900. Many of the cottages in the centre of the village were owned by the Heaths of Kitlands. George Heath bought Kitlands in 1823 and during the next thirty years he added to the property by buying the farms of Moorhurst, Trouts and Anstie Grange.

Roffey's shop, Coldharbour, *c.* 1905. This seventeenth-century building was for many years the shop and post office run by Henry Roffey, who also provided refreshments at the base of Leith Hill Tower. At its busiest times the shop employed a dozen people as assistants, delivery men and counter clerks.

The post office, Coldharbour, *c.* 1940. The Roffey family had been trading in the area since at least 1862 and it was a major change in the village when Henry Roffey's shop closed and a new shop and post office were built on the other side of the road in 1938 and run by Miss L. Weller.

Christ Church and the vicarage, Coldharbour, *c.* 1910. Built in 1848 in the Early English style by John Labouchere of Broome Hall, the church was on a site given by the Duke of Norfolk. The heads on the corbels over the east window outside depict John Labouchere and his wife. The vicarage is now a private residence, as Coldharbour now shares a vicar with Abinger.

Coldharbour, *c.* 1905. The iron room was built by Mr Pennington of Broome Hall in 1893 principally as a reading room. There was a small library and daily papers were provided together with 'illustrated and comic papers'. Visitors were free to use the room at what was considered to be a trifling fee. Behind the reading room was a recreation room and the two were occasionally thrown into one for concerts and village entertainments.

The infants' school was formerly housed in a wooden building on the site of Mr Smith's shop until John Labouchere, an earlier owner of Broome Hall, sanctioned the building of the school shown here, in 1851.

Henry Roffey's shop, *c.* 1900. At the time this photograph was taken Henry Roffey, the Coldharbour shopkeeper, proclaimed on his signboard 'established over 100 years', but not at this building. Closer inspection of the signboard reveals the words 'and at Coldharbour', but despite fairly extensive searching the location of this shop remains a mystery.

Leith Hill, *c*. 1910. Erosion caused by walkers is evidently not a new thing. The tower was very popular with Victorian and Edwardian visitors, so much so that the Coldharbour shopkeeper Henry Roffey ran a refreshments tent there during the summer. Sir Samuel Romilly, a famous judge who lived at nearby Tanhurst, recalled the rejoicings that took place after the defeat of Napoleon in 1814: 'From Leith Hill we saw, on Easter Tuesday (14 April) at night, the lights of the illuminations of London on account of the recent events in Paris.'

Leith Hill and Hotel, *c*. 1920. The 64 ft tower sits atop Leith Hill, behind the house of the man who had it built, Richard Hull. Construction took place in 1765, with the battlements and external stair turret added in 1864.

'Leith Hill, like Box Hill, has been used as a place of sepulchres. At its foot is a residence called Leith Hill Place, which rather more than a century since was inhabited by a Mr Hull. He built the tower which now crowns the summit of the hill, and left orders in his will that he be buried within it. These instructions were carried out, and the tower thus became what it has always remained – a tomb.' (E.A. Judges: *Some West Surrey Villages*, 1901)

Leith Hill Tower, *c.* 1908. 'Here we may sit upon short soft grass or thicker heather, and gaze over miles and miles of country far below us. All the land seems mapped out in squares of various hues, divided by green lines. Here a golden patch denotes the harvest approaches; there is a square of green with little brown and white dots upon it, which must be oxen grazing.' (*Dorking and Neighbourhood*, 1888)

DORKING & MICKLEHAM

Dorking Mill (Castle Mill), c. 1912. There was a mill at this site recorded in Domesday and in 1760 it became part of the Betchworth Castle Estate. George Dewdney, whose family were tenants from 1743 to 1849, added stables, outbuildings and a tenement, and also enlarged the mill in 1836. A trade magazine advertised the mill lease in 1883 as 'a water corn-mill with four pairs of stones with convenient storerooms and other outbuildings together with fifteen acres of very productive meadow land. An excellent residence and two cottages. On the River Mole with an unfailing supply of water. Present tenant has been in possession for twenty years and there is an extensive retail and grist trade.'

W.H. Atkinson purchased the freehold from the Denbies Estate in 1921 for £1,600. After a fire in 1933 the mill was much reduced and was only making animal feed from one of the four pairs of stones until production ceased completely in 1952. The mill was restored in the 1970s and became a private dwelling. Happily, the mill-wheel still turns, although purely for the pleasure of its owners and passers-by on the nearby footpath.

Castle Mill, Dorking, c. 1920. The mill and house are just out of the picture, to the left. Dorking's River Swimming Club had its bathing house here, rented for 1s p.a. from the Hope Estate, and its half-mile race had taken place annually since 1870. When it closed in 1940 it was one of the oldest of its kind in the country.

The Watermill, Dorking, c. 1930. A late Victorian building situated high above Castle Mill, one of Dorking's very old watermills, this has been variously a café, restaurant, tea-rooms and night club. On the right of the picture can be seen the open-air swimming pool with its blue fountain showpiece; it was Dorking's only swimming pool after the closure of the public baths in Station Road in 1939. The Watermill's pool closed in the 1950s after an undetectable leak, and is now merely part of its car park.

Box Hill Bridge, Dorking, *c.* 1914. The A25 was carried over the River Mole by this bridge, opposite the entrance to Betchworth Park Golf Club, until the new stretch of road, including Deepdene Bridge, was opened in 1927. The old bridge was severely damaged in floods in 1968 and has now been replaced by a metal footbridge.

Castle Gardens, Dorking, *c.* 1880. The former stable block to Betchworth Castle was designed by Sir John Soane and built in 1798. It was developed into houses after the sale of the Deepdene Estate in the 1920s and is now a Grade II listed building. (Photo: J. Chaplin)

Pixham Lane, Dorking, *c.* 1905. In 1884 an iron room was erected at the junction of Leslie Road. It served as a Sunday school, mothers' meeting room, night school ('in the winter twice a week for big lads who liked to keep up what they had learnt at school') and Bible class. It was badly ventilated and, like all iron rooms, was very hot in summer, cold in winter and in constant need of repair. In 1903 it was replaced by the present Lutyens-designed church, which is dedicated to the memory of the two brothers of benefactress Mary Mayo.

Leslie Road, Dorking, *c.* 1928. Mary Mayo recalled: 'There was a path leading from Pixham Lane to the Castle Mill across a very pretty meadow. It belonged to Shrub Hill, and when the whole estate was sold in 1881, Mr Butcher bought this portion and laid it out in plots for 40–50 cottages, now Leslie Road and Riverside.'

    The Leslie family owned Shrub Hill, which stood along the southern side of the High Street taking in the stretch between Paper Mews and the Surrey Yeoman. Only a small portion of the house remains, hidden by the present shop fronts. In 1810 Baron Leslie became Earl Rothes and his daughter, Lady Elizabeth Jane, married Capt. Augustus Wathen, names that are now recorded on street maps of the town.

Box Hill station, Dorking *c*. 1908. In 1849 the Reading, Guildford and Reigate Railway opened its line from Redhill through to Guildford with a station at the north-western end of the town, including a goods yard, called Dorking Town (now Dorking West). A second station, Box Hill, was opened in 1851 and is now called Deepdene.

Reigate Road, Dorking, *c*. 1935. In about 1912 a blacksmith's shop stood in front of this house at the junction of the Reigate and London roads, but it was demolished to improve visibility for fast-increasing road traffic. The house itself was taken down in about 1937 when the site was acquired for the Gaumont (later Embassy) Cinema. The Telephone Exchange and car parking for the council offices now occupy this site.

The Punchbowl Inn, Dorking, *c.* 1910. This splendidly proportioned inn, built of local stone, was designed by Sir John Soane in 1789, but unfortunately in 1971 (and later) it was extended and is virtually unrecognisable as the pretty little roadside inn of 200 years ago.

Lonsdale House, Dorking, *c.* 1900. This house stood in East Street (now High Street) facing Moores Road, and was demolished in 1936 to make way for New Parade.

'Here a substantial Dutch-looking mansion, which probably remembers the third William, there a tasteless structure which was put up in the days of the next of his name, here perhaps a house that may go back to the days of the Restoration, there a spick-and-span Victorian erection, which affects Gothicism or Queen Anne-ism or something else which is unreal, but still falls in fairly well with the general irregularity.' (E.A. Judges: *Some West Surrey Villages*, 1901) (Photo: J. Chaplin)

Deepdene, Dorking, *c.* 1880. The magnificent mansion Deepdene House, designed and built by Thomas Hope, Henry Hope and William Atkinson between 1818 and 1840, was one of Dorking's architectural gems. Tragically it was demolished in 1969. The two round-topped brick structures in the foreground were apparently ice-houses for the mansion. (Photo: J. Chaplin)

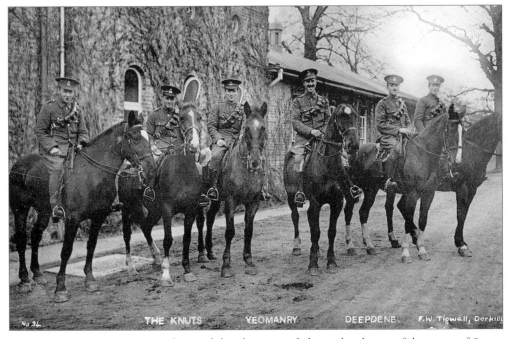

Deepdene, *c.* 1915. No amount of research has thrown any light on the identity of this group of Surrey Yeomanry billetted at Deepdene House during the First World War. It was common practice for soldiers to give their company nicknames, but why The Knuts?

High Street, Dorking, *c.* 1870. An unusually empty High Street with just two boys standing near the Three Tuns public house, now demolished. A little further along stands the Black Horse, also demolished. Both of these public houses were used by market traders to clinch deals, thus avoiding the fees charged at the Thursday Market. Further down the street, on the southern side, no building has yet taken place beyond the Surrey Yeoman, that land still belonging to Shrub Hill House. The posts supporting the sunblinds mark the bounds of market rights. Traders could display their wares within these areas on market days.

'The streets were metalled with flints drawn either from Ranmore or Bradley Farm. They were carted to the wide roadside verge on the Westcott Road, just west of the Pound (Sandy Lane) and there two or three men with quite small hammers could be seen all day during the summer months breaking the flints to a more or less standard size. In the autumn the stone was drawn into the town in tip-carts and shot down into heaps and roughly spread. The local Highway's Board road roller, a stone one drawn by a horse, flattened down the worst of the flints and the traffic was left to do the rest. It was surprising what large ruts in the newly laid metals the 3 or 4 inch iron-shod wheels of a heavily laden waggon could make.' (Dr W. Hooper: *Notes on Dorking for the Surrey Archaeological Society*, 1945) (Photo: J. Chaplin)

High Street, Dorking, *c.* 1870. A delivery cart stands outside the Red Lion Family Hotel, which in the mid-1800s had its own brewery run by W. Breem & Co., advertising 'Families supplied with mild and bitter ales of every description . . . delivered to Sutton, Tooting and south-west London.' The ghostly figure of a young girl in the left foreground is evidence of the relatively long exposure times needed for glass plates of this date. (Photo: J. Chaplin)

High Street, Dorking, *c.* 1903. Deliveries of ale are being made to the Three Tuns, on the far left, and there is still not a motor vehicle to be seen. The Red Lion, on the right, has become a 'family and commercial Hotel' with a new porch over the steps. It was from these steps that James Broadwood JP, of Lyne House, Capel, sought to quell an agitated crowd of farm labourers, many of whom were on the verge of starvation after a failed harvest in 1830, who had gathered to protest at poor pay and conditions of the farm hand. Broadwood failed and the crowd fought with police and cavalry until the Riot Act was read from the same hotel steps. The ringleaders of the gang were transported. The Red Lion was demolished in 1964.

High Street, Dorking, *c.* 1870. On the spot where the NatWest Bank now stands was a building used by Misses Ann and Ellen Agate for their gift shop. Mr Dinnage recalled: 'Next to Chequers Yard was a shop that, as a boy, I could never pass without a long gaze at the window. It was the leading toyshop of the town, kept by Miss Agate. All the choice toys of the day were to be seen, and inside was a perfect fairyland to youngsters. Huge rocking-horses, targets for archery, cricket bats, toy pop-guns, and toys of all descriptions were discernible in the recesses and background of the shop. One used every device to get inside the shop to catch a fleeting sight of the delectable display.'

On the right is the office of J. & W. Attlee, 'millers (water), maltsters and corn dealers. Parsonage and Pixham Mills. Agents for Phoenix Fire Insurance.' (Photo: J. Chaplin)

High Street, Dorking, *c*. 1870. The Philps family had been trading in Dorking without a break since 1623. Clara (b. 1859) was the last member of that family business, which was listed in 1862 as 'tailor and woolstapler', and before her death in 1949 she recalled in her unpublished memoirs: 'All the property at the back was called Plumms. It was copyhold and we paid 6*d* to the Duke of Norfolk for it. It had meadows and fields and orchards at the back. My great grand-father was a fell-monger, he dressed skins. When I was a child the garden was where the skins were dressed. My father had a great wool-room at the back of the dwelling house. There were two sheds where the wool was stacked. The fleeces were packed in large sacks about 6 ft by 4 ft with a hole in the middle. Into these, the fleeces were packed, the hole sewn up, and the sacks sent chiefly to London. The wool-room was packed tightly with fleeces, when full, a trap door was opened, a crane with two grappling irons swung them out and dropped them into place.' (Photo: J. Chaplin)

High Street, Dorking, *c.* 1870. This fine photograph by J. Chaplin of Guildford depicts Dorking as many contemporary writers record it, a busy, bustling market town. Thursday was market day, when, as Clara Philps recalled, 'there were pens from the streets on the cobbles. Cattle were tied to the railings. Pigs and chickens and rabbits were on the cobbles on the other side. On Fair Day (Holy Thursday) they used to race horses up and down the street.'

The last street market was held in 1926. The large, ornate clock mounted over the pavement (centre left) was over the premises belonging to Thomas Wood, described in 1867 as 'retail and family grocer, Italian warehouseman and cheese monger'. At that time he also had premises in Station Road described as 'tallow chandler', and the sign-writing above the High Street shop proclaims 'candle factory'. (Photo: J. Chaplin)

High Street, Dorking, *c.* 1870. The Wheatsheaf (left) used to have a circular cock-fighting pit in the cellar and in 1750 its landlord, Mr Philps, achieved fame for rearing what was said to be the largest hog ever seen in England, weighing in at 1,036 lb. The inn closed in the 1970s and has been well restored for use as a bookshop. Next to the Wheatsheaf stands Maybank's, wine and spirit merchants, in the building that Miss Philps described as 'the original bank'. Certainly the fine porticos intimate a rather superior entrance.

Dr W. Hooper described the road surface as being a problem. 'In summer dust was a plague and in winter the mud was bog-like. In the High Street there were three paved granite pedestrian crossings and these were kept clean by the Local Board roadmen using metal and rubber scrapers. (Photo: J. Chaplin)

West Street, Dorking, *c.* 1950. This area is renowned these days for its proliferation of antique shops but before the 1970s it had almost the complete set of 'butcher, baker and candlestick maker': Woods had a candle factory in Station Road, there was a bakery at 1a and a butcher's nearby. Now that the road is one way only, many of the old trades have given up, including the Neptune Fish Café on the left of the photograph.

West Street, Dorking, *c.* 1910. The approach route into the town from the west, along the A25, remains much the same today as it was at the turn of the century. 'In West Street is the Public Hall erected in 1872 by a local company, and at its rear, but forming part of the same block are what used to be dwelling-houses, built after the Peabody style though now converted into a set of offices. The room underneath the Hall is used as a coffee and refreshment room and a series of religious meetings are continually being held here under the presidency of Lady Hope (Miss Cotton).' (*Dorking and Neighbourhood*, 1888)

West Street, Dorking, *c.* 1870. Clarendon House was largely rebuilt in the eighteenth century by Resta Patching Jnr, and for a period it was the Mathematical and Commercial School for Boys. Saved from demolition in the 1980s, it is now offices. (Photo: J. Chaplin)

Rose Hill, Dorking, *c.* 1870. This pretty development of Italianate and Tudor-style villas was built between 1838 and 1860 in the grounds of Rose Hill House. (Photo: J. Chaplin)

Rose Hill Archway, looking towards Rose Hill, *c.* 1870. '. . . under the archway is Rose Hill, a collection of neatly-built residences, encircling a large meadow, most of them owned by the British Land Company, and kept very select; so much so, that anything in the shape of a business is entirely excluded.' (*Dorking and Neighbourhood*, 1888) (Photo: J. Chaplin)

South Street, Dorking, *c.* 1930. This is how the street appeared after the widening scheme of 1920 had removed some old shops and houses that stood near to the bandstand, which itself was removed in the 1960s. Just visible through the bandstand is the early nineteenth-century Rotunda described in *Dorking and Neighbourhood* thus: 'In South Street is a large building called the Rotunda, formerly used as a natural history museum, but now cleared of its curiosities and utilized as a warehouse.'

South Street, Dorking, *c.* 1910. Little change has taken place to these buildings along the southern end of South Street. F. W. Mays, the long established car dealer, has a showroom just on the left of the photograph, beyond the two cottages; the main showroom and garage is behind the photographer.

South Street and Horsham Road, Dorking, *c.* 1935. In front of the Queen's Head, with its fine mansard roof, is a 'stop-me-and-buy-one' ice-cream seller, and beyond is the bus garage. Towards the end of 1930 a house named Townfield with an acre of ground was purchased by the East Surrey Traction Company, and work subsequently began on a building for forty vehicles and a coach/bus station on the forecourt. Complete with a 6,000 gallon underground fuel tank the building opened in 1932 with the proposal of employment for 160 men. The garage closed in 1990, was demolished soon after and apartments built in its place.

St Paul's Church, Dorking, *c.* 1870. Benjamin Ferrey designed this Anglican church, which was completed in 1857, with a south aisle being added in 1869. 'The district church of St Paul stands out prominently, with the beautiful domain of Denbies in the background, whilst to the right are Polesden, Norbury Park and Box Hill, all adding to the effective landscape. On entering the Glory Wood . . . a profuse growth of blackberry and other bushes covers the ground, and these form a great attraction to lovers of that delicious fruit. Many varieties of beautiful ferns were, years ago, to be found here but the ruthless hand of the fern gatherer has torn them from their woodland home and carried them to the London markets.' (*Dorking and Neighbourhood*, 1888) (Photo: J. Chaplin)

The Cottage Hospital, Dorking, *c.* 1870. The site in South Terrace was granted at a peppercorn rent by Mrs A.A. Hope of Deepdene and building was completed by 1871. Voluntary contributions supported the seven beds and three cots that the hospital offered. 'The cottage hospital is in this district and a healthier spot could not have been selected for the purpose to which it is devoted.' (*Dorking and Neighbourhood*, 1888) (Photo: J. Chaplin)

South Terrace, Dorking, *c.* 1870. Of the large middle-class villas built in Dorking at this period, these two are fine examples: Burchet House (left), for a time a girls' school, and Harrowlands; both are now gone. (Photo: J. Chaplin)

Howard Road, Dorking, *c.* 1870. (Photo: J. Chaplin)

Looking across the lower slopes of Ranmore, with Denbies, the mansion built by Thomas Cubitt in the early 1850s, just visible on the crest, *c.* 1880. The mansion was demolished in 1953. The slopes of Ranmore are now planted with grapevines belonging to Denbies Wine Estate. (Photo: J. Chaplin)

St Martin's Church, Dorking, *c.* 1870. This so-called Intermediate Parish church was completed in 1837 to the designs of William McIntosh Brookes. It was described by a contemporary writer as 'one of the most unsightly churches ever built. A tall spire towered above the belfry placed over the chancel, encased in copper sheathing; but the interior had such a cold cheerless aspect about it that in 1865, preparations were made for replacing it by a nobler edifice.' (*Dorking and Neighbourhood*, 1888)

Already a new chancel has been erected, and by 1874 the nave and tower followed in the same style. (Photo: J. Chaplin)

Meadowbank, c. 1870. Meadowbank House was a substantial fifteen-roomed family home with formal gardens laid out with Wellingtonias, Scots pines, a tennis lawn, orchards, kitchen gardens and stabling for five horses. Standing in 29 acres, it was part of Cubitt Estates Ltd until Dorking Urban District Council purchased the site in 1926 for £6,750 with the intention of providing a recreation ground and building homes on the remainder. By 1932 the western half of the land was again for sale after the council had decided not to encumber itself with the cost of a building programme. The property was bought by Maurice Chance, a former chairman of the council, who subsequently sold it to a developer at which time Meadowbank House was demolished and the Parkway Estate was constructed. In 1953, to mark the Festival of Britain, the council built a new stadium in Meadowbank for the Dorking Football Club and the ground was opened by Football Association secretary Sir Stanley Rous. (Photo: J. Chaplin)

From Bradley Farm, *c.* 1870. It is possible that the Bradley Estate was a 'sub manor' of Dorchinges, mentioned in the Domesday Survey of 1086 and later purchased by the Sondes family in the fifteenth century. Latterly it was absorbed into the 3,900 acre Denbies Estate, which sold off sections close to the railways in 1921 on which were built the large houses comprising Keppel and Calvert Roads. (Photo: J. Chaplin)

Dorking, *c.* 1870. On the right of the picture can be seen Dorking Town station, built in 1849, to the left of which are cattle pens. Just visible, centre left, is the so-called Intermediate Parish church. (Photo: J. Chaplin)

Church Street, Dorking, *c.* 1865. This very early photograph by J. Chaplin shows, possibly, all the residents of the row of 1820s houses leading up to the Intermediate Parish church. There are two etched bricks in the entrance to Archway Place reading 'JB 1827' and 'JW 1827'. (Photo: J. Chaplin)

Burford Bridge Hotel, Dorking, *c.* 1910. Formerly known as the Fox and Hounds, this inn was a haven for well-known figures of the day, some of whom would have been visitors to George Meredith's chalet, in the garden of his house, Flint Cottage, just along the zig-zags. Rebuilt and extended in 1935 and the 1970s, the hotel now boasts a fine seventeenth-century tithe barn transported from Abinger Manor. E.A. Judges described the inn in 1901 in *Some West Surrey Villages*: 'At the pretty little house called the Fox and Hounds in the valley of the Mole, beneath the western slope of Box Hill, Keats wrote the latter part of his poem "Endymion".'

Holden's Rest, Box Hill, *c.* 1910. With the advent of the railway connection to London and its suburbs, and with the introduction in 1871 of Bank Holidays, majestic scenery such as that around Box Hill attracted thousands of day trippers. Refreshments had been provided at one or two locations on the summit since 1901.

The Flats, Box Hill, *c.* 1908. J.S. Ogilvy wrote in *A Pilgrimage in Surrey* (1914): 'In 1797 all the box trees over 20 years growth upon the Hill were sold to Messrs Nicholson & Hoskins for £10,000, not more than 380 tons to be cut in one year. This shows that a much greater area of timber must have existed than is the case now. The enterprise proved ruinous from over-production, and we may be glad that it did so, otherwise the Hill would have lost one of its most characteristic features.'

Donkeys on Box Hill, *c.* 1910. For the London visitor, no day trip to Box Hill was complete without a donkey ride. The area at the summit, close to the look-out, is now called Donkey Green. The National Trust acquired its first portion of Box Hill in 1913 from Sir Leopold Salomons of Norbury Park, who bequeathed the land to the nation.

Chalkpit Cottages, Mickleham, *c.* 1912. The main Dorking to Leatherhead road was but a narrow country lane at this time, and it was not until 1937 that the growth in road traffic necessitated its widening into a dual carriageway with cycle paths on either side. The cottages in the foreground are now gone. The old Roman road, Stane Street, made its way north from Chichester, through Ockley and Dorking to the ford at Burford Bridge, and then by Mickleham Church into Ermyn Street, 'in reality a narrow lane or bridle-path continuing from Mickleham Church towards Ashtead Park'. (Ellen Smith)

Bytton Hill, Mickleham. The road on the right leads up to the William IV public house, built in 1830, and continues round to the National School, which opened in 1843. Standing on the ridge at the left of the picture are the almshouses, which are built around the Poorhouse, which was constructed in 1789. This had become redundant by the 1830s and was dilapidated until Sir George Talbot offered a sum of money for repairs. A trust was established and the building was converted into six sets of two-room dwellings and Bytton Cottage. After a fire in 1864, architect Charles Driver and the builder William Spicer reconstructed the complex, which comprised eight sets of rooms. A little further along the main road lay the old forge, which survived into the 1950s as a café for lorry drivers.

FOREST GREEN, OCKLEY & OAKWOOD HILL

St Margaret's Church, Ockley, from Ockley Court Farm, looking south, c. 1904. The first reference to the church is in 1291. In 1302 the right was granted to hold a market on Tuesdays, and a fair each year on 20 July, the festival of St Margaret of Antioch. As no remains of an earlier building have been found, and as the present building dates from this period, it would seem probable that it was the first church to be built on this site. The south wall of the original nave dates from 1300, the porch from 1400, and the tower and bells from 1700, making them the oldest complete peal in Surrey. In 1872 the north aisle and vestry were added and the chancel rebuilt. The pond has long since been filled in.

The Old Hatch and the King's Arms, Ockley, *c.* 1920. The sixteenth-century Old Hatch faces the King's Arms, which is seventeenth-century with nineteenth-century additions. The storage buildings to the right of the inn were to become Worsfold's Garage in 1920, which is reputed to have owned the first motor car in the village. The site was cleared in 1969 and a pair of houses stands there now.

Ockley Green, *c.* 1904. The pump was given to the village in 1837 by Jane Scott, a governess to the Arbuthnot family of Elderslie. A handsome oak-framed canopy of Horsham stone slabs was originally supported by four columns of Leith Hill stone with cushion capitals. Unfortunately some of these were damaged in 1985 by a car and all the columns have now been replaced. Water of excellent quality was reportedly obtained from the 70 ft deep well drawn by an iron pump, removed in 1965.

'We think we may say of Ockley that it is one of the prettiest villages we have seen. The houses are dotted about round a village green upon which, if we come on a summer's evening, we shall probably see the major portion of the inhabitants, some enjoying a game of cricket, the others acting the role of spectators.' (*Dorking and Neighbourhood*, 1888)

Ockley drapery shop, *c.* 1920. The eighteenth-century Surrey House was the home to the Surrey Trading Company in the 1920s, which was run by Miss Stone, chiefly as a haberdashery. To the left is the seventeenth-century building that was formerly the bakery but is now the stores and post office.

Stane Street, Ockley, *c.* 1905. This view is taken from outside the Old Schoolhouse, once Ockley Academy for about fifty boys between 1810 and 1860, after which time it was used for non-conformist religious gatherings. It became a guest house in 1918.

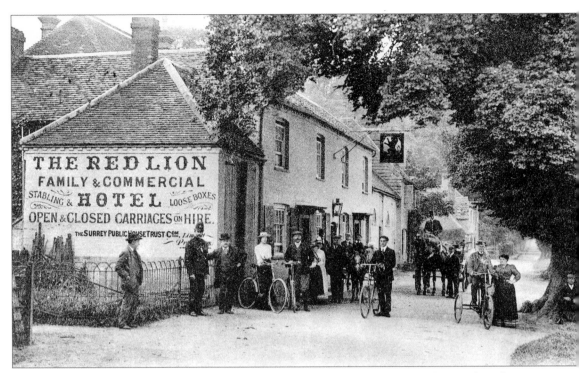

The Red Lion, Ockley, *c.* 1905. This is a fine example of the photographic work carried out by Percy Lloyd of Albury. The group of people, with mixed modes of transportation, stand under one of the famous avenues of trees that lined Stane Street until recent years. The seventeenth-century Red Lion was, at this time, owned by the Surrey Public House Trust Company, which was later to become Trust House Forte.

The pretty little village school was another gift (along with the village pump) from Miss Jane Scott and was opened in 1841. Comprising one classroom and a teacher's house, the sandstone building soon proved too small and was enlarged in the 1870s. In the 1990s it became 'federated' with Capel School and the two schools are now known as the Scott-Broadwood School. On the right is the former St John's Church, built in 1872 and declared redundant in 1983. It was converted into dwellings by Ansells of Ockley who had constructed it for £880 over one hundred years earlier.

Elderslie, *c.* 1910. J.S. Ogilvy, in his *A Pilgrimage in Surrey* written in 1914, described Ockley thus: 'In this part of Surrey the yeomen and husbandmen have always been persons of consequence. There are no houses of any antiquity but many farmhouses are large and important buildings, which until comparatively recent times were still owned by families whose ancestors were there before the Norman Conquest, and it is possible that the one large house among the picturesque cottages of the village occupies the site of one of these. It is now apparently a house of early eighteenth-century date, and has long been occupied by members of the Arbuthnot family.'

Ockley Windmill, *c.* 1921. Aylmer's or Elmer's Mill was built in 1803 for Robert Harrison at a cost of £735. This large octagonal smock-mill was used to grind corn for the large local houses of Jayes, Ockley Court and Broome Hall until 1905. The fabric of the building rapidly deteriorated in disuse and the whole structure collapsed in 1944 leaving the stone base, which stands today. The farm barn to the right in the picture is now a dwelling.

'No doubt the windmill has been burned down many times since the Crusades, and it is rapidly falling into decay now; but it is all complete and exploration of the interior right up to the top, where the great cog-wheels transmit the power of the sails to the upright driving shaft, suggests that the miller has merely gone home for the night and left the door open. The slats rattle in the frosty evening wind and the great sails groan at their moorings as if they would fain be loose again and doing the work they have done so long.' (J.S. Ogilvy: *A Pilgrimage in Surrey*, 1914)

The Old Schoolhouse, *c.* 1910. This early seventeenth-century building is one of the most recent public houses in the village, having received its licence in 1965 after the closure of the Brewery Arms, an old ale-house situated a little further along Stane Street. From 1810 to 1860 the building housed the Ockley Academy for Boys; it subsequently became a meeting-house, a guest-house, tea-rooms and most recently a sea-food restaurant.

Leith Vale, Ockley, *c.* 1902. Called Leith Hill Lodge originally and built by the Hadley family in 1740, the house was sold to their cousins, the Cowper-Browns, one branch of whom lived in nearby Standon Homestead. The Sunday school at Okewood Church was erected in memory of Emma Cowper-Brown in 1890. Richard Trotter, a treasurer of the Royal Horticultural Society, added to the house extensively in the 1930s and employed six gardeners to tend the grounds. It is said that when he left in 1950, he took three lorry loads of plants with him. The next owners acquired the house, 27 acres, five cottages and Black and White Cottage, and set their sights upon harvesting the mature oaks until anxious neighbours alerted the authorities and preservation orders were granted. The present owners, the Inglis-Jones, acquired the property in 1965.

Jayes, *c.* 1910. A hunt meeting at Jayes showing the house before the addition of the octagonal library at the southern end in 1913. In the 1866 edition of *Walks and Drives Around Dorking* the writer says 'The mansion known as Jayes is the seat of Lee Steere Esq. It is fronted by a beautiful and nicely timbered park, at the bottom of which is a lake whose surface is seldom rippled except by the majestic sailing of the timorous swan. The manor, which in the time of the Conqueror was held by Richard de Tonbridge, is now in the possession of Lee Steere Esq., who is the representative of a family of great antiquity and supports the character of an English gentleman with the genuine spirit of English hospitality.'

Oakwood Hill, the view towards Ockley from the recreation ground, *c.* 1910. J.S. Ogilvy recalls seeing a rural tradition near the church in the early 1900s. 'Near the path by which I had reached the chapel, there was a little crowd assembled as if for an auction sale; now I found that these were the candidates for the bread-dole, given, I think, by one of the Evelyns, to be distributed on a certain day about Easter. None of these women were very clear about its origin, but, so far as I could learn, there was very little ceremony beyond regulating the quantities according to the number of the applicant's children.'

Oakwood Hill, *c.* 1920. The Punchbowl Inn was once divided into two parts, with the landlord's accommodation separate, as shown here. J.S. Ogilvy is a little dismissive of the village's charm: 'There is nothing in the hamlet of Oakwood Hill except one or two picturesque cottages and a roadside tavern, though there is a pretty little landscape at the north end where the road crosses the brook.'

Hale Cottage, Oakwood Hill, *c.* 1930. This pair of farm workers' cottages were situated in a hollow opposite Hale House on the road to Ockley. Part of the Jayes Estate, they were demolished in the 1960s after being declared uneconomical to repair.

St John the Baptist's Church, Okewood, *c.* 1910. This isolated, beautiful church was built in about 1220 for 'ye inhabitants of ye outborders of ye parysshes of Wotton, Okley, Abinger, Rydewyke, Warnham and Ewhurst in ye county of Surrey and Sussex . . . which dwelle very ffar dystant from ye parryshe churches.' Let into the old chancel floor is a small brass recording the death of Edward de la Hale in 1431, who restored and enlarged the chapel and also endowed it with lands. In the eighteenth century the condition of the chapel was so deplorable that two neighbouring yeomen took the matter in hand, sold three of the bells, raised a further £8 and had some buttresses erected which saved the chapel from complete collapse. Major restoration took place in 1879, and in 1997 another programme of works commenced.

The Parrot Inn, Forest Green, *c.* 1920. The building has been standing for at least 400 years. An 1840 map shows the Parrot Inn with a tea garden on the opposite side of the road on the green. In recent times the inn was, for many years, leased by Surrey Trust Houses as a free house with two tiny bedrooms for bed and breakfast guests at 3*s* 6*d* per night.

The forge, Forest Green, *c.* 1905. There has been a smithy on this site for 150 years, and in the early 1900s there was a baker's shop next door. The buildings were totally renovated in the 1990s, providing the forge with a showroom for its fine quality products.

Holy Trinity Church, Forest Green, *c.* 1905. This little church was dedicated in 1897 by the Suffragan Bishop of Southampton, having been built as a memorial to Everard, son of Charles Hensley of nearby Pratsham Grange, who was shot by his cousin while out hunting rabbits in 1892.

Forest Green, *c.* 1915. The village first appears as an entity in 1580 when it was called Folles Green and later, in the same document, as Forrest, Ferless, Farleyes and Farleys Green.

Congregational chapel, Forest Green, *c.* 1910. The chapel was built in 1877, twenty years earlier than Holy Trinity Church, and was in continual use for eighty years. It was then converted into use as an artist's studio, and is now designated thus on maps.

Forest Green Stores, *c.* 1905. The busy stores and post office were run by the Jays, Worsfolds, Stringers, Cuthberts, and finally the Whites, until the business was no longer viable and went the way of scores of village shops, closing in the 1980s. The building is once more a private house.

Forest Green, *c.* 1920. C.R. Stringer ran the shop and post office at this time, and although motor cars were being seen more often, cattle still grazed the green unfettered. The triangular green of 26 acres had always been an integral part of community life, and Queen Victoria's Diamond Jubilee probably saw the most frenetic activity. The celebrations started with a married versus singles cricket match; dinner for 150 people was served in St Barnabas's Mission Room (built in 1887 at the corner of Tillie's Farm but later destroyed by fire); sports and games followed; then tea for the mothers and children and prizes presented at 6 p.m. by Mrs Hensley. At dusk rockets were let off, and at 10 p.m. the bonfire was lit.

THE HOLMWOODS

North Holmwood, c. 1910. At the junction of Holmesdale Road and Spook Hill stands the Dorking Brick Company's manager's house and office. This Victorian building was altered and extended in the 1930s as a showcase for the company's brick products. The pit closed in the 1960s and the site was used for housing in the 1980s.

North Holmwood, *c.* 1903. The common land was grazed by cattle, horses, donkeys, goats and geese for centuries, but as the large houses were built so portions of common land were enclosed. Bracken was cut for use as animal bedding, and any person who wished to claim an area assembled at 6 a.m. on 25 August to mark out the desired area by placing small heaps of cut bracken every 10 yd.

North Holmwood, *c.* 1910. Spook Hill rises on the left, lined by Sefton Villas, the late Victorian development. On the horizon can just be seen Tower Hill House. Trees have now grown in the foreground, obscuring this viewpoint.

North Holmwood, *c.* 1910. The general store known as The Cabin was also a tea room at this time, and on the right stands Dorking Brick Company's office at the corner of Holmesdale Road.

St John's Church, North Holmwood, *c.* 1916. North Holmwood became an Ecclesiastical District by an Order of Council on 6 August 1874, at which time the building of a new church commenced on a site given by the Duke of Norfolk who owned the land until 1956, when care of the common was handed over to Dorking UDC. This role is now fulfilled by the National Trust.

Holmwood Common, *c.* 1915. These three substantial houses on Holmwood Common are Braeside, Holly Cottage and Ferndale. Almost completely surrounded by woodland now, they are reached from Mill Lane.

Holmwood Common, *c.* 1910. Eutrie House was built in 1860 for the Chaldecot family and was then called Meadow Lodge. During the Second World War Eutrie House was on the Secret List and acted as a wireless receiving/transmitting post, large antennae having been erected in the grounds.

Holmwood Common, *c*. 1910. Moor Lodge was built in 1875 and was originally called Moor Cottage. It was for some time Dr Robinson's surgery; he is reported to have been one of the first owners of a motor car in Holmwood.

Holmwood Common, *c*. 1870. This early photograph was probably taken from the western side of the A24, and looks across to the Charter Mill, which was demolished in 1873. It is very difficult to be exact about the viewpoint because so many trees now obscure the scene. (Photo: J. Chaplin)

Holmwood Park, *c.* 1917. In 1830 Mr Seymour Larpent bought 120 acres of the common from the Lord of the Manor and built Holmwood House, later called Holmwood Park. Mrs Larpent's sisters, the Misses Arnold, built Holmwood Cottage, on the right of the picture, around a 1750 dairy farm. To the left are the stable buildings. The Larpents were great benefactors of the village, funding the building of the vicarage, school and contributing towards the building of St Mary Magdalene Church.

Mid-Holmwood, looking across Bond's Pond to the A24, *c.* 1910. On the other side of the road can be seen the Old Nag's Head (in the centre of the photograph). On the far right, Priory Cottage is situated on the site of the old Mission Hall.

Folly Farm, South Holmwood, *c.* 1910. Folly Farm was tenanted at this time by W. Barker, who also ran the butcher's shop at Aberdeen House. Milk was delivered twice a day to the village from Folly Farm.

Holmwood (Charter) Mill, *c.* 1870. Taken by J. Chaplin of Guildford, this rare photograph depicts the Charter Mill shortly before it was demolished. This post mill had been working since about 1700, the last miller being Mr Strudwick, who lived in a house to the rear of the Sawyers Arms (later the Holly and Laurel).

Fourways or Fourwents Pond, South Holmwood, *c.* 1920. This popular beauty spot, at the junction of four roads, was reportedly enlarged in 1876 to allow the watering of horses of the 3,000 troops who were encamped in the grounds of Capel Leyse for a Troop Review by the Duke of Cambridge.

South Holmwood, *c.* 1920. Betchett's Green Lane forms part of one of the earliest settlements within Holmwood, Betchett Green Farm being of sixteenth-century origin and Betchett Green Cottage dating to about 1595. The pond has recently been restored by the National Trust.

South Holmwood, *c.* 1910. Cricket had been played on this ground for more than 100 years until it fell victim to a road widening scheme during the 1960s. On the left of the picture is Barker's butcher's shop, the wooden building in front being the slaughterhouse.

South Holmwood, *c.* 1930. The Holly and Laurel was formerly the Sawyers Arms, and stands on the site of a wayside ale-house dating back to 1662.

South Holmwood, *c*. 1910. On the right is the Strict Baptist chapel built in 1874 and now a private residence, while next door is Laburnum Cottage, which was the telephone exchange until the late 1920s. The post office proudly bore the telephone number Holmwood 1, and it was to take thirty-five years before the numbers had reached 88.

The Norfolk Arms, South Holmwood, *c*. 1919. For many years the Norfolk Arms was the meeting place for local organisations taking part in the great annual Church Parade. After processing along the road to the church for the service at 3 p.m., the parade would return to the Norfolk Arms for tea. At the rear of the property stood Harry Isemonger's workshop, where walking sticks were made.

Norfolk Garage, *c.* 1930. Frank Pierce had worked from the Norfolk Arms as a fly proprietor at the turn of the century with a range of carriages from Tally-Hos to Victorias. These were replaced by motor cars in the 1920s and the garage was established, proudly boasting a Sunbeam and a Model T Ford for hire. Stanley Pierce took over the business in 1930 and is seen at the centre of the photograph, flanked by mechanic Ben Batchelor and Frank Pierce. These buildings were knocked down in 1956 and a new garage was completed in 1957. This is currently occupied by a tractor company.

Norfolk Arms, South Holmwood, *c.* 1904. Landlord Charles Taylor with his wife and daughter, Minnie, stand at the front door. The pub was the focal point for most village festivities, and for many years the Ancient Order of Foresters Friendly Society met here. During the Second World War soldiers billetted at the Norfolk Arms burnt all the banners, furniture and regalia of the Foresters, no doubt in an effort to keep warm.

South Holmwood, a scene of rural idyll looking across the lazy A24 to the church, *c.* 1905. On the right is George Croft's bakery and post office, with the wooden building on the left housing the fire pump. To the right of the picture is Mrs Baxter's haberdashery shop.

South Holmwood, *c.* 1900. Villagers stroll contentedly along the main road while boys play with a cart down Betchett's Green Lane.

The Church of St Mary Magdalene, South Holmwood, *c.* 1907. This church was built in 1838 from local stone and was funded chiefly by Mrs Larpent of Holmwood Park. In 1914 enlargements to the chancel were made and a new east window was constructed in 1914. Revd J. Utterton was the first vicar, and went on to become Bishop of Winchester in 1851.

The vicarage, South Holmwood, *c.* 1903. The vicarage was built in 1839, funded by Mrs Larpent of Holmwood Park, and sold in 1966. A new smaller vicarage was subsequently built in a portion of the old kitchen garden.

South Holmwood, *c.* 1911. The building of the school in 1844 was also funded by Mrs Larpent, and the first headmaster, Mr Bixby, had 150 pupils under his charge in six classrooms. In about 1900 night schools were introduced to teach boys carpentry and gardening, and girls needlework. 'A very superior building and fortunately better endowed than such village schools usually are; so that the staff of teachers is of a superior kind.' (*Dorking and Neighbourhood*, 1888)

South Holmwood, *c.* 1917. Warwick Road and the Village Hall (built in 1906). Strong & Sons plumbers and decorators yard can be seen on the left; this was later the premises of A. Hoad & Sons, coal merchants. These buildings were demolished in the 1970s to make way for a pair of houses.

LEIGH & NEWDIGATE

Gardeners, Burys Court, c. 1910. Dressed alike and eminently suitably for their profession, they are wearing stout leather footwear and long baize aprons tied around the waist. Gertrude Jekyll wrote of 'fashion' in 1904: 'For real working clothes, like all other things that are right and fit for their purpose, never look shabby. They may be soil-stained; they may be well-worn, but they never have that sordid, shameful, degraded appearance of the shoddy modern Sunday suit put to an inappropriate use.'

Leigh Place, *c.* 1910. In early times there were two principal houses in Leigh: Leigh Place and the manor house of Shellwood. The first reference to a house on the site is in a conveyance from Sir John Dudley in 1527, and part of Leigh Place may have been in existence then. The house appears to have become dilapidated in the latter half of the sixteenth century and it is probable that extensive alterations were made then. A large part of the house was pulled down in 1810. The building is chiefly unaltered today, except that the brickwork is now bare again.

Mynthurst, Leigh, *c.* 1905. This late Victorian mansion, built for Sir Henry Bell, was described by Pevsner as 'Big and very ugly Victorian Tudor. Symmetrical brick and stone with a west tower.' The house is now divided into apartments.

Clayhill Road, Leigh, looking north towards the village green, *c.* 1910. The pair of late Victorian farm workers' cottages on the right are now one dwelling, and just beyond on the right a small row of council houses was built in the late 1940s; along with other small sets of houses these were the first changes to this once entirely agricultural community, whose population in 1901 numbered 541.

The Green, Leigh, *c.* 1905. The 'old' school on the left was opened in 1846 to accommodate forty boys and forty girls. At this time it was fee paying with pupils contributing *2d* per week, the balance being met by subscriptions. Expenses were estimated to be £50 per annum.

The vicarage, Leigh, *c*. 1905. This eighteenth-century building stood in an acre of ground on the piece of land across the green from St Bartholomew's Church. It was destroyed by fire in the 1970s and replaced by dwellings for the elderly, named Harrington Close after a former long-serving chairman of the parish council, Walter Harrington.

The green and schools, Leigh, *c*. 1905. The 1846 school building was enlarged in 1884, making a larger main room and making the school house, in part, into an infants' room. A new school house was built comprising two bedrooms, sitting room and kitchen. A sitting room and bedroom were provided for the assistant teachers in a part of the old school house.

The well on the green was dug in 1875.

Leigh School, *c.* 1909. Mr A.E. Tickner, headmaster, stands with his charges, probably for the last time on this site, because they moved to the 'new' school in Tapner's Road in 1910. An entry in the *Holmesdale Directory* for 1907 reads: 'The village attained considerable notoriety in 1905 on account of the alleged insanitary condition of its schools, where some improvements have since been carried out.'

School Log, 1864: 'March 9th. Weather extremely wet, brooks unpassable. Small attendance of scholars. March 21st. Several children absent being engaged in bean-planting.'

Leigh school, *c.* 1920. The 'new' school was opened in 1919, offering three classrooms, a large hall and playing grounds. A fence separated the boys' playing area from the girls', and each side had its own six-cubicle toilet block. During the summer months the boys walked along the roadside to the recreation ground to play cricket, and after a particularly hot match they queued up for a drink from a solitary tap that stood by the main gate.

The Plough Inn, Leigh, *c.* 1910. The oldest part of this inn on the village green is probably seventeenth-century, with Victorian additions. The outbuilding on the left, by the roadside, was used at one time to house a travelling wagon, from which meat was sold, there being no butcher's shop. The hounds are probably the Old Surrey and Burstow pack.

The green, Leigh, *c.* 1910. This is a typically English village green, where stands a pump, an inn and a grocery store. Behind the pump is Chantry Cottage, which boasts two remaining bays of a medieval building to which has been added a new front facing the green, an outshot to the south-east and a lean-to to the south. It is possible that this was an ecclesiastical building, housing perhaps a chantry priest or nuns.

The village stores, Leigh, *c.* 1900. The shop and house adjoining were added to Chantry Cottage in the 1800s and stand on the site of Church Grove Farm. In 1910 the freehold was advertised thus: 'A desirable block of property with double frontages. It comprises a dwelling house and shop, three bedrooms, general shop, sitting room, kitchen, scullery and warehouse to which is attached the Post and Telegraph Office. Also detached gig house and two pigstyes, front garden and orchard. £30 per annum.' The lot sold for £140. Miss Gurney ran the shop from the late 1930s until about 1953, at which time the post office moved to Duthill in Dawes Green, whereupon Mrs Rice became postmistress. A new shop opened at Evered in Clayhill Road, run by Mr Fairman.

The village stores, Leigh, *c.* 1900. On the left, standing in front of Gurney's shop, is well-known local figure 'Doker' Weller, who for many years lovingly tended the cricket ground.

St Bartholomew's Church, Leigh, *c.* 1885. This rare photograph shows St Bartholomew's before the Victorians altered it in 1890. The nave was lengthened, a new west entrance and porch constructed and the original squat tower was crowned with an oak shingled spire. The photograph also shows clearly the three simple cottages that were knocked down in the early 1900s.

St Bartholomew's Church, Leigh, *c.* 1900. It is seen here after the alterations of 1890 and bears little resemblance to its earlier fifteenth-century counterpart. The three cottages next door were demolished soon after this photograph was taken. To the right are the three old cottages that form the central portion of the large house now called Priest's House.

The forge, Leigh, 1907. Standing by Forge Cottage are Mr Parsons (shopkeeper before Miss Gurney) and Mrs Flint, and in the foreground are Mr Salmon (blacksmith, who lived at Thyme Cottage) and Mr George Flint (tenant of the forge), who died in 1910. His son Frank took over the forge, which soon became a garage and petrol station, also running a taxi service from 1929 to 1953. His daughter Nellie and her husband George Livermore ran the petrol station until the 1970s when their son Roy took it over, ending the family connection with the business in the 1980s when the house and garage were sold.

Smallholdings, Leigh, *c.* 1915. There were many of these council-owned smallholdings in the village at this time. Alfred and Eliza Wheatley moved into St Joan in 1928 with their three girls, Edie, Daisy and Nell. With eight cows grazing 25 acres, the daily milk yield of 10–15 gallons was delivered by bicycle to the village and on to South Park and Reigate. The morning's milking started at 4 a.m. with an afternoon session at 3 p.m. To the left of St Joan lived the Clements and Harringtons while to the right lived the Hattons and the Paines. On the opposite side, at Rosemary, lived Charlie Hunt the fishmonger, whose wife sold dry goods such as tea and sugar. This house later became Mrs Bonwick's tea house, which was very popular with cyclists but was demolished in the 1980s.

Flanchford Mill, Leigh, *c.* 1910. This predominantly wooden mill is of a type now very scarce in the south-east of England; the first reference to it was made in the thirteenth century, when it was called Flansford Mill. There is an etched brick in the pit floor dated 1768 which indicates that the estate owner, James Scowen, was probably the builder of the mill. In 1863 Charles Dowlen from Parsonage Mill in Dorking was the miller here and he fitted a new wheel, of the wooden breastshot type, in 1870. Edward Elphick, a wealthy corn merchant with premises in Reigate, took over the mill in 1887, with Mr Bartlett being the last miller in the 1900s. By the Second World War the mill had ceased functioning and is currently in a dilapidated state.

Shellwood Mill, Leigh, *c.* 1890. This is believed to be the only photograph in existence of this large post mill. Built in about 1770 and tenanted by William Batchelor for the rent of 'two good fat capons to be delivered at Christmas to the Lord's mansion', the mill was burnt down and replaced by a larger-than-average example in 1795 by James Bowyer, It was said to stand out as a 'landmark for some miles', with its four double-shuttered patent sweeps. William Kempshall learnt to mill and dress stones at Shellwood before going to work for Bowyer at Wonham watermill in 1884. The mill was described in 1911 as 'that somewhat rare survival in these times, a working windmill' (*Victoria County History of Surrey*). The body of the mill was demolished in 1920 and the roundhouse in 1936.

Paige's van, *c.* 1940. A bakery was set up after the demise of Shellwood Mill with its bakery. Arthur Wicks was still trading from Shellwood as miller and baker in 1907. Edward Paige was the baker at Dawes Green from the 1930s. Standing on the right is Henry Baker, bread boy, who lived at Shellwood Mill.

St Peter's Church, Newdigate. Standing on the site of a twelfth-century chapel is the stone church with a timber tower, dating from the fifteenth century. By 1830 the building was said to be in bad repair but it was not until 1877 that major repairs and alterations were instigated by the Revd Lancelot Studdert-Kennedy, resulting in a new north aisle being added and the porch rebuilt. In 1985 the tower was renovated and a specialist in the craft of oak shingling was eventually traced who trained some local men to cut and replace the worn shingles. A pillar near the door has crosses carved into it, and local legend has it that these were made by Knights Templar off to the Crusades, from their nearby property at Temple Elfold in Capel which they owned until 1308.

St Peter's Church belfry, c. 1906. The timber tower dating from the early fifteenth century is supported by four enormous 17 inch-square timbers standing upon wooden slabs. This postcard was sent by a craftsman working on the church in 1906, and the message reads: 'Dear wife, I was pleased to hear from you today, sorry about Mr H. I have to call at office and from there I shall go to Miller's. I don't suppose I shall be home much before half-past nine. Don't keep any dinner about. I will get something on the road. This is part of the Tower we have started on, it is a very interesting church, especially the Tower, there are only about half doz. examples in England. Will tell you all the news when I see you. Love from Bimma.' It was addressed to Islip, 44 Granville Street, Peterboro.

The Schoolhouse, Newdigate, *c.* 1905. The 'new' endowed school was opened in 1872, replacing the 1838 building provided by J.S. Broadwood. Initially there was provision for fifty pupils under the tutelage of Henry Hackwood, schoolmaster until 1910. By 1904 the number of pupils attending the school had risen to forty-seven boys and forty-nine girls with three members of staff: Ellen Chandler, pupil teacher, receiving £35 p.a.; Mrs Rusbridge, infant teacher, receiving £57 10*s* 0*d*; and Henry Hackwood receiving £140 p.a. This school was demolished in 1964 and some flats for the elderly were built on the site, named after the former churchwarden, bellringer and Parish Council Chairman George Horley who died in 1974.

School pond, Newdigate, *c.* 1926. Sometimes called Church Road, School Lane or Burnt Oak Road, this lane runs alongside the church, past the site of the 1872 school, which is now replaced by dwellings called George Horley Place. In 1903 the Parish Council decided that motor cars should not exceed 8 m.p.h. 'from the Kingsland Road to Tanhurst, from the church to Cudworth, and from the shop corner to Parkgate'. Down the lane, on the right, is Dean House Farm, the oldest part of which dates to 1630.

Newdigate Place, *c.* 1905. It was built in 1897 for city wool merchant George Herron, who named his new mansion Newdigate Place despite the fact that there was already a house with this name. The older dwelling was renamed Home Farm. The new Newdigate Place featured a splendid staircase and some fine panelling worked by Herron's wife Ellen, a gifted wood-carver. It was she who started evening classes in the subject in 1902 because 'at that time there were no socials or dances . . . nothing to do but loaf about and hang around Mr Dean's shop window for the sake of the lamplight, and choir practice for those in the choir'. After the Second World War the house fell into disrepair, and was sold for building materials for £1,150 in 1954.

Congregational Mission Chapel, *c.* 1910. In 1817 the non-conformist family called Risbridger took the tenancy of Gaterounds, where Joseph began to hold services, and from 1876 open-air services were held at the Congregational Mission in Parkgate, established by the Dorking minister, the Revd J.S. Bright. The iron Mission Hall was opened in July 1885, and attracted a large gathering who listened to the preaching of Newman Hall and Revd Bright. The chapel flourished for many years, but as numbers fell the chapel closed its doors in the 1960s. In recent years it was used as a scout hut, but that usage ended in the 1980s.

The Surrey Oaks, Newdigate, *c.* 1900. This building was originally a simple timber-framed, two-bay cottage, probably dating to the seventeenth century. In 1779 the building is recorded as being a wheelwright's workshop and was not officially an inn until 1851, with Mary Butcher as licensee and her son William still working as a wheelwright. By 1881, however, the building was trading solely as an inn, and by the turn of the century the name the Surrey Oaks was being used.

The Six Bells, Newdigate, *c.* 1920. This eighteenth-century building stands on the site of an earlier inn, and until the church had a sixth bell hung in 1805, the inn was named the Five Bells. In 1801 Mrs Waller is recorded as being the landlady, succeeded by Mr Cheesman, Mr King and Mr Penfold in 1822. At some stage, G. J. Butcher ran both the Six Bells and the Surrey Oaks.

The Six Bells, *c.* 1920. Members of the Surrey Union Hunt pose for a photograph in front of the Six Bells before embarking on a clay-pigeon shoot.

Six Bells Cottages, Newdigate, 1921. Built around a sixteenth-century four-bay house with seventeenth-century additions, the dwellings are known today as Old Cottage and White Cottage, the former being originally known as Hasteds and the latter being a public house known as the Wheatsheaf in about 1840.

BIBLIOGRAPHY

Baker, Kathleen, *Forest Green*, Portcullis Press Ltd.

Berry-Clarke, James, *The Parish of Ockley in Surrey* (1989).

Bird, Margaret, *Holmbury St Mary, one hundred years* (1979).

Capel and Beare Green Magazine (1967, 1973, 1976, 1980).

Dodson, K.M., *Birth of a Parish, Christ Church, Brockham* (1988).

Dorking and Neighbourhood – a handy guide to rambles in the district, T. Fisher Unwin (1888).

Farries, K.G., and Mason, M.T., *The Windmills of Surrey and Inner London*, Charles Skilton Ltd (1966).

Harding, Joan, and Banks, Joyce, *Newdigate, its history and houses* (1993).

Holmbury Parish News.

Hooper, Dr W., *Notes on Dorking for the Surrey Archaeological Society* (1945).

Jackson, Alan, *Dorking, a Surrey market town through twenty centuries,* Dorking Local History Group (1991).

Jekyll, Gertrude, *Old West Surrey,* Kohler & Coombes, Dorking (1978).

Judges, E.A. *Some West Surrey Villages*, Surrey Times Printing & Publishing Co. Ltd (1901).

Mayo, M., *Pixham 1862–1912.*

Memories of Old Dorking, Kohler & Coombes, Dorking.

Nash, William, *A Surrey Memory of 1851*, Kohler & Coombes, Dorking.

Newdigate Society, *Newdigate Guide.*

O'Kelly, Terence, *The Villages of Abinger Common and Wotton, Surrey* (1988).

Ogilvy, J.S., *A Pilgrimage in Surrey,* Geo. Routledge & Sons Ltd (1914).

Rideout E., Lawrence, J., and Collins, Revd M., *The Ockley Visitor.*

Ryan, Meg, *Betchworth Within Living Memory* (1988).

Sheppard, R. *Micklam, The Story of a Parish*, Mickleham Publications.

Smith, Bill, *A Surrey Village – Coldharbour* (1985).

Smith, Bill, *A Surrey Village – The Holmwood* (1983).

Smith, Ellen, *The Reigate sheet of the one inch Ordnance Survey.* Adam & Charles Black (1910).

Stanway, Revd O., BA, *The Story of Okewood Church.*

Stidder, Derek, *The Watermills of Surrey*, Barracuda Books (1990).

Sturley, Mark, *The Breweries and Public Houses of Guildford, Part II* (1995).

University of London, *Victoria County History of Surrey* (1911).

Walks, Rides and Drives around Dorking – Companionable Guide to the Town and Neighbourhood, R.J. Clark, Dorking (1866).

Watney, John, FSA, *Some Accounts of Leigh Place, Surrey, and its owners*, Roworth & Co. Ltd (1893).